1242

Praying

☐ CHRISTIAN SPIRITUALITY SERIES ☐

Remember Me
Praying the Jesus Prayer
Life's Changing Seasons

Praying The Bible

Imagination in Bible Meditation

Brother Ramon SSF

Marshall Pickering

Marshall Morgan and Scott
3 Beggarwood Lane, Basingstoke, Hants RG23 7LP, UK

Copyright ©1988 by Marshall Morgan and Scott Publications Ltd
First published in 1988 by Marshall Morgan and Scott Publications Ltd
Part of the Marshall Pickering Holdings Group
A subsidiary of the Zondervan Corporation

British Library CIP Data
Ramon, *Brother*
    Praying the Bible – (Evangelical Spirituality Series)
    1. Bible. N.T. Gospels – Meditations
    I. Title II. Series
242'.5   BS2555.4
    ISBN 0 – 551 – 01544 – 6

Text set in Baskerville by Brian Robinson, Buckingham
Printed in Great Britain by Henry Ling Ltd,
at the Dorset Press, Dorchester, Dorset

Contents

'Invocation' Charles Wesley   7

Introduction: The Scripture, the Spirit, the Community   9

1 Preparation   The Interior Indwelling of the
Holy Spirit   13

2 Inspiration: The Spirit's Fire in the Word
of Scripture   17
The Power of the Word

3 Imagination: The Awakening of the Mind and Heart   21
Definition of Imagination
Imagination and Scripture
Imagination must be Sanctified
Imaginative Illustration

4 Meditation: Deeper into Prayer   33
Varieties of Method
Illustrative Old Testament Passages
The Flowering of the New Testament
Companying with Jesus
Setting about it:
     1. Relaxation
     2. Respiration
     3. Visualisation
     4. Participation
     5. Adoration
Letting it Happen
The Meditation
Reflection

5 **Contemplation:**   The Spirit in Control   55
                       The Vocation to Comtemplative
                       Prayer
                       Spiritual Depth
6 **Communication:**   The Overflowing Gospel Life   60

Conclusion: Pulling the Threads Together   62

Author's Note

The masculine pronoun is used in a generic, not an exclusivist, sense throughout.

Invocation

Come, Holy Ghost, our hearts inspire;
   Let us Thine influence prove,
Source of the old prophetic fire,
   Fountain of light and love.

Come, Holy Ghost, for moved by Thee
   The prophets wrote and spoke;
Unlock the truth, Thyself the key,
   Unseal the sacred Book.

Expand Thy wings, celestial Dove,
   Brood o'er our nature's night;
On our disordered spirits move,
   And let there now be light.

God, through Himself, we then shall know
   If Thou within us shine,
And sound, with all Thy saints below,
   The depths of love divine.

Charles Wesley

Introduction

Scripture, the Spirit, the Community

This book is about praying the bible. It is meant, first of all,
for those who have been reading the bible for years, who have a
fair understanding of its broad teaching and implications in the
areas of christian doctrine and life, but who have never really
been able to 'get into' scripture in their life of prayer.

Secondly, it is for those who give lip-service to the inspiration
of scripture – even hold rigid and dogmatic views about biblical
authority, but in truth do not spend time in quiet mediation,
and never break the shell to discover the sweet kernel of
scripture.

Thirdly, it is for those Christians who are always seeking
something novel, exciting, stimulating, exhilarating – caught
up in the restless spirit of the times. They are described by
A.W. Tozer: 'We read our chapter, have our short devotions
and rush away, hoping to make up for our deep inward
bankruptcy by attending another gospel meeting or listening to
another thrilling story told by a religious adventurer lately
returned from afar.'

Fourthly, it is directed to those who have cultivated an
interior and imaginative life of quiet and prayer, who have a
sense of God's presence in nature, art, poetry, music and other
aesthetic and religious dimensions, but who have never given
themselves to the meditative study of scripture.

I am not proposing an intellectual, liturgical or doctrinal
study of the bible, nor am I recommending a perusal of the life
and teaching of Jesus for purposes of information or homiletical
communication. What I am really concerned about is that we

develop, cultivate and sustain a prayerful and meditative openness to the written word, so that the Holy Spirit may awaken, activate and stimulate our imaginative vision. We shall then enter into actual awareness of, and communion with, Christ.

If we were simple, loving, open and contemplative human beings, as God would have us be, this would be the simplest thing in the world, and the most natural. But as it is, such simplicity is immensely difficult for us. We are more capable of cerebration than celebration, and though study is difficult for many of us, we still find it easier than a childlike attitude of wonder, passive receptivity and openness to the word and Spirit of God.

It will not be enough to share my own experience, to impart advice and counsel, or to clarify our thinking about the whole procedure. We must also get down to *practise* scripture meditation, to learn to offer our imaginative faculties of vision and creative thought, and in the Holy Spirit to give ourselves to the meditative savouring of scripture, leading into contemplative prayer.

Of course, scripture is not the product of an individual, and it must not be interpreted in an individualistic manner. Neither must it be subjected merely to human reason, for the nature of inspiration is that it contains hidden treasure only to be revealed to the pure heart and illumined mind. It is the product of the community of faith, and must be read within the fellowship of the community. The same Holy Spirit who inspired the word illuminates the eye of the heart, and the Holy Spirit means us to understand scripture both in an evangelical and catholic sense. The evangelical sense of scripture implies the personal relationship of penitence and faith, the joy and assurance of sins forgiven and of life in Christ. The catholic sense ensures that the personal does not lead to individualism, but leads to the corporate sharing within the fellowship of the whole Church. We are not saved alone, though our experience may be intensely personal. 'A threefold cord is not quickly broken', says the book of Proverbs, and our threefold cord has a strong binding unity of purpose. The three strands are Scripture, the Spirit and the Church. We should be able to stand within the fellowship of the Church, with the bible in our hands, and the Spirit in our hearts, and in this way we shall learn a deeper, corporate way of biblical prayer in the Spirit, being delivered from subjective fantasies, intellectual sterility and exclusivist fanaticism.

1: Preparation

The Interior Indwelling of the Holy Spirit

There are many things to say about the Holy Spirit, but the two primary things that are the work of the Spirit are both objective and subjective. His work is without and within the spirit of man. Objectively, the Holy Spirit indwells the created order because he is 'the Lord and Lifegiver', and the inspirer of the prophets and apostles, whose witness and writings are enshrined in the canon of scripture.

Subjectively, the Holy Spirit moves within the human spirit, continuing to inspire all that is good, true and holy in our lives. There is a certain finality and givenness about the inspiration of scripture because it is the authoritative norm for the Christian Church, but the work of inspiration has continued corporately and individually down through the ages. All subjective and personal inspiration is to be measured and checked by the objective canon of scripture and the mind of the Church. But that does not limit the free and spontaneous exhuberance of prophecy and illumination, for the Lord has yet more light and truth to break forth from his word. I shall go on to expand the meaning of objective inspiration in the next section, but here I want to affirm the interior indwelling of the Holy Spirit, for that is a prerequisite for an understanding of scripture or a practice of christian prayer.

The Holy Spirit was active both in creation and redemption in the Old Testament, but the intimate and interior indwelling of the Spirit was only glimpsed and promised in those days of legal obedience. The great prophets understood from afar and to some extent anticipated the wonder of such indwelling, for

Jeremiah could prophesy: 'This is the covenant which I will make with the house of Israel, says the Lord: I will put my law within them, and I will write it upon their hearts; and I will be their God, and they shall be my people.' And the promise was intimately connected with the Holy Spirit in the vision of Ezekiel: 'A new heart will I give you, and a new spirit I will put within you; and I will take out of your flesh the heart of stone and give you a heart of flesh. And I will put my spirit within you . . .'

These are the prophetic promises which were fulfilled first of all when God became incarnate in the person of Jesus of Nazareth. He was not only born of the Holy Spirit, but was anointed and filled with that same Spirit for his works of healing and ministry. He laid down his life in the power of the Holy Spirit and was raised from the dead by the Spirit of holiness. He was not only the Suffering Servant of Isaiah's prophecy, but also the Temple of God in which the shekinah glory of God shone with great radiance.

He revealed himself to his disciples after the resurrection and breathed on them, saying: 'Receive the Holy Spirit . . .' and on the day of Pentecost, Mary his mother, surrounded by the apostles and disciples, numbering one hundred and twenty, were filled with the Holy Spirit, and thus the prophetic promises of the old covenant were fulfilled, and the old prophetic fire burned in the New Testament Church.

This is the inheritance into which every Christian enters at baptism and conversion, and the interior indwelling of the Holy Spirit is that inner light and witness which is given for illumination and contemplation, leading to knowledge, love and holiness of life. These are the basic truths which are the foundation of the christian life of love and prayer, and should lead the believer into an ever-deepening awareness of contemplative prayer through meditation upon the scriptures and communion with God.

The Holy Spirit's energies are not confined to the redemptive work of salvation and religious conversion, of course. They extend to all the creative impulses and dynamic revealed in all the arts and sciences. There is nothing in the world of nature or of the creative faculties which are devoid of his life-giving power and beauty, but it is not our present task to trace his presence and power in all that is true and good and life-giving, but to draw attention to his redemptive indwelling in the believing Christian, and his prophetic illumination in the believer's and the Church's understanding of scripture.

The important thing is not to rush to the written word, exercising all the powers of brain and intellect of natural reason and scholastic training, for in doing so, many have missed the *spirit* of scripture, and far from being illumined by the Holy Spirit, they have found the bible to be dry bones, devoid of marrow and life. As in the visiion of Ezekiel, only the Spirit can give life in the valley of dry bones, only the Spirit can subjectively awaken in the believer's heart the objective value and power which resides in the written word, so that the living Word can be discovered in the treasure-house of scripture.

It is by the moving power of the indwelling Spirit that I am moved to prayer, to tears, to joy, to love. It is the indwelling Spirit who fills my heart with longing, stimulates me to creativity, lifts my soul in response to music, to poetry, to all artistic forms and energies. The same Spirit fills me with joy, with sympathy, with compassion for men and women around me in need of friendship, of dialogue, of help and healing. He is the Spirit of life, so I recognise his presence in the soil, in the sea, in the sky, in the sun, moon and stars. He is the Spirit of wholeness, so I feel him in beauty, in symmetry, in balance, harmony and sound bodies and minds. He is the Spirit of truth, so I appreciate his presence in intellectual pursuits, academic excellence, and all the scientific and artistic disciplines of the mind and heart. He is the Spirit of forgiveness and healing, so I experience, greet and recognise him in all acts of forgiveness, all procedures and sciences of medicine and recuperative endeavour. In my christian pilgrimage, I understand the old negro song which cries out:

> Every time I feel the Spirit
> Moving in my heart, I pray . . .

for when the Spirit moves then I am moved; when the Spirit struggles within me, than I am held, activated, subdued and energised, and prayer is born in the deepest depths of my heart.

There are whole dimensions of truth to explore in tracing the Holy Spirit's work and influence in all the works of nature and grace, but we are concerned with the interior work of the Spirit in the life of prayer as we come to holy scripture. So now we turn to the moving of the Spirit in the inspiration of the sacred word.

2: Inspiration

The Spirit's Fire in the Word of Scripture

Inspiration is a rare word in the New Testament, occurring only once, in 2 Timothy 3:16, in relation to scripture, but it is a powerful analogy, and its implications are found throughout scripture. The reference reads: 'All scripture is inspired by God and profitable for teaching, for reproof, for correction, and training in righteousness . . .' The Greek word *theopneustia* means *God-breathed*, and the reference is to God breathing into man's nostrils the breath of life, and man becoming a living soul in Genesis 2:7. The breath of God, both in Old and New Testaments, is the Holy Spirit, for the Hebrew *ruach* and the Greek *pneuma* both mean *spirit, wind* and *breath*. It is this inspiration of God that breathes throughout creation, bringing life and fertility wherever it blows, and sustaining animate life in man and beast. The same breath of God breathes in redemption, and both his life-giving power and illuminating fire and light are celebrated in the Wesleyan hymn quoted at the beginning of this book.

Another key text is found in 2 Peter 1:21, which also includes an apostolic warning that only the Spirit who inspired the scriptures can interpret them aright: 'No prophecy of scripture is a matter of one's own interpretation, because no prophecy ever came by the impulse of man, but men moved by the Holy Spirit spoke from God.' The Greek verb rendered *moved* by the Holy Spirit literally means being *borne along*, and the same verb is used in Acts 27:15,17, where the ship in which Paul travels is *borne along* by the wind. As a ship is borne along on the sea by the power of the wind, so the prophet is borne along by the

Holy Spirit, not communicating a private opinion of his own, but a revelation given by God. The context is not only that the prophet is carried by the inspiring Spirit of truth, unfolding God's revelation, but also that the interpretation of that revelation needs the illumination of the same Spirit. No man has the right to interpret for himself, but must heed the discipline and wisdom of the wider Church. This does not refer to the passing fancies of any contemporary commentator, subjecting scripture to the critical judgment of the passing age, nor to the exclusivist and heretical sects which are mushrooming in our days, but to the disciplined understanding of the historic Church upon doctrines of fundamental importance, with freedom in the matters which are secondary.

The Catechism of the American Episcopal Church asks: 'How do we understand the meaning of the Bible?' And the answer is given: 'We understand the meaning of the Bible by the help of the Holy Spirit who guides the Church in the true interpretation of the Scriptures.' Charles Wesley understood this clearly, as evidenced by the stanza:

> God, through Himself, we then shall know
>> If Thou within us shine,
> And sound, with all Thy saints below,
>> The depths of love divine.

This is not, of course, to disregard scholarship in favour of some kind of mystical intuition of an esoteric kind. The reverse is true. Hidden, esoteric mysticisms must be suspect in favour of disciplined and dedicated scholarship through which the Holy Spirit can work in interpretation, reinterpretation and application in every age. Scripture is not interpreted by private and biased cleverness, nor by prejudice toward an esoteric sect or cult, but in the light of the Spirit's work in the catholicity of the Church, for spiritual things are spiritually discerned. We all have our pet foibles and doctrines, not always rooted in scripture, and many of us would like to alter and mould the canon of scripture to our own ends, whether we are Anglicans or Catholics, Pentecostals or Presbyterians, Baptists or Quakers. We are all under the authority of scripture, within the fellowship of the wider Church.

The Power of the Word

I am not, of course, arguing for a literalist, fundamentalist understanding of scripture, for violence, destruction and bloodshed have been buttressed by the quotation of scripture, and it is salutary to note that nearly all the heretical cults and sects affirm a plenary inspiration of scripture, and at the same time deny the divinity of Christ, and therefore the Incarnation and the Holy Trinity. But neither am I arguing a blind submission to an infallible Church. Calvin is often more biblical than those who followed him, and at the beginning of the *Institutes* he writes of the inner testimony of the Holy Spirit to the word of scripture:

> Those whom the Holy Spirit has inwardly taught truly rest upon Scripture, and that Scripture indeed is self-authenticated; hence it is not right to subject it to proof and reasoning. And the certainty it deserves with us, it attains by the testimony of the Spirit. For even if it wins reverence for itself by its own majesty, it seriously affects us only when it is sealed upon our hearts through the Spirit.

The prophet of old, like the apostle, was burdened with the word of God. Jeremiah cried out because the fire of God burned in his bones, and the psalmist was aware of the searing flame of inspiration within him. Amos was not in the line of the prophets, nor had he any prophetic training, but God called him powerfully, and he makes it very clear: 'The lion hath roared, who will not fear? The Lord God hath spoken, who can but prophesy?' There was no choice, it was a holy burning, a divine compulsion, and if it brought loneliness, rejection and persecution, then so be it. Jeremiah spells it out:

O Lord, thou hast deceived me, and I was deceived.
Thou art stronger than I, and thou hast prevailed.
I have become a laughingstock all the day; everyone
   mocks me . . .
For the word of the Lord has become for me
   a reproach and derision all day long.
If I say, 'I will not mention him, or speak any more
   in his name,'
There is in my heart as it were a burning fire shut
   in my bones,
and I am weary with holding it in, and I cannot.

Throughout the bible, the analogies used for the word of God are all effective instruments for powerful truth. The word of God is a fire that burns, a hammer that strikes, a sword that cuts. It is manna that feeds, milk that sustains, and meat that strengthens. The Hebrew *dabar* meant not only *a word* but *a thing*, and when the *dabar-Yahweh*, the word of the Lord, goes from his mouth, it actually *does* something, it accomplishes God's will, it does not fail in its purpose. The prophetic word is like an arrow, a spear, a sword that pierces, cuts and wounds the hardened sinner and hypocrite, but heals and sustains the repentant sinner who is wounded by the divine love.

What I have been maintaining here is the twofold inspiration of the Spirit – the divine power by which the word is begotten in the mind and heart of the prophet and apostle – that is objective inspiration – and the inward illumination which takes place in the enlightened mind and heart of the believer – that is subjective inspiration. Holy Scripture stands as the authoritative written word, objectively inspired by the Holy Spirit, and the believer who is open to the interior illumination and subjective inspiration of the Spirit is the one who is led deeper into the life of meditation and prayer.

Let us turn now to the work of the Spirit in illumining the sinner and awakening the imagination as the letter of scripture becomes the inspired word to the believing heart.

3: Imagination

The Awakening of the Mind and Heart

Such has been the influence of negative doctrines of the fall of man in the western Church, with its concept of total depravity, that in both catholic and protestant theology there has been a fear of all the creative faculties of man's nature. It is true that we are all tainted by fallenness, and in our unregenerate and alienated condition we cannot, unaided, find our way to God. But by the grace and love of God, though the *imago Dei*, the image of God, has been broken and defaced, yet there are traces and echoes of that divine image within us. That means that the imagination of man, though it may be tainted, and turns frequently to evil, yet is also capable of intellectual truth and aesthetic beauty, for the Holy Spirit continues his creative work. And certainly, in the heart and mind of man regenerated and redeemed, there is a new flowering of the creative imagination, giving rise to a restored Eden with all the flowers and fruits of loveliness and fertility. I am arguing for the restoration of the divine image in man, and for a redeemed and sanctified imagination in the life of theology and prayer.

A young man came to the monastery the other day suffering from a psychological and spiritual frustration, together with some depression which he had come to talk about, because members of a religious group he had been associating with had told him that he was not to use his imagination and not to read any writings that stimulated his imagination. One of the books that was proscribed was J.R. Tolkien's *Lord of the Rings*. I wonder what their evaluation of Bunyan's *Pilgrim's Progress* would have been, quite apart from the tremendous amount of

21

imaginative and creative prose, poetry, liturgy and hymnology of the Church down through the ages. The diverse literary traditions of the Old Testament are full of imaginative power, and Jesus continually appealed to the imagination of his hearers in story, parable and analogy.

Not only do the creative powers of the imagination meet us in the scriptures of the Old and New Testaments, and in the psalmody, liturgy, homilies, poetry and hymnody of the Church, but God intends us to use our sanctified imagination in learning, teaching, communicating at every level, and especially in the mediative life of prayer. This is an area in which, grounded in scripture, we are able to enter into story, parable, analogy and healing miracle, and find ourselves planted right in the midst of scripture 'as if we were there', and in that way we can be there, sharing in all the blessings of forgiveness, reconciliation and healing. The negro sprital hymn understands this powerfully:

> Were you there when they crucified my Lord?
> Were you there when they crucified my Lord?
> Oh . . . sometimes it causes me to tremble, tremble . . .
> Were you there when they crucified my Lord?

The believer follows Jesus to the cross and to the tomb; suffering with him, dying with him, rising with him, and waiting for his coming in glory. It is the sanctified power of the imagination by the Holy Spirit, so that scripture is made real in the experience of the praying, believing soul.

Definition of Imagination

When we talk about imagination, just what do we mean? Well there are a number of ways of defining it:

a I form a mental concept of what is not present to the senses: eg. I imagine myself in the vision of the valley of dry bones with Ezekiel (ch. 37);

b I visualise a situation or dimension which is not yet in existence for me: eg. I think of my resurrection body in heaven, based upon the transfiguration and resurrection of Jesus;

c I visually place myself in a situation in which I am not physically present: eg. with the saints and martyrs who suffered for Christ (Hebrews ch. 11) or with believers suffering today under a totalitarian regime;

d I visualise dimensions of existence and experience which are now only potentially possible by faith: eg. healing miracles in my own experience, or the Second Coming of Christ to transform the whole created order.

It is not a question of *whether* we should use our imagination in our approach to scripture, but *how* it should be used, what are the positive uses of the imagination, and what kind of warnings should be sounded against the negative use of the imagination. Imagination is a faculty that is neutral in itself – like the reasoning and intuitive faculties. These, like the imagination, are part of the wholeness of our being, and are basic to intellectual knowledge and intuitive wisdom which provide for us the human experience which leads us into maturity and compassion in our realtionships with the world and with other people.

Of course, imagination can be prostituted, it can become obsessive, it can lead us into a negative or sensual world of fantasy which feeds the lower and sensual parts of our nature. On the one hand, it is a valuable experience to read the classic novels which lead us into worlds and cultures which are both familiar and unfamiliar to us, rich in imaginative expression of the lives and experiences of the inter-relationship of people and events. There is an added value in the high literary quality of such novels, and the blending of good literature and excellence of literary expression stimulates the positive and active use of the imaginative faculty. On the other hand, novels which stimulate erotic, manipulative and sadistic desires, whatever their literary quality, pander to a prostitution of the noble faculty of imagination. It is, of course, difficult sometimes to categorise, for there is a wealth of imaginative material which is of good literary quality, which may be required reading for education and professional qualifications, but which can be of dubious moral influence to certain kinds of people.

I do not intend to be legalistic about the application of this principle, but the point I am making is clear: the imagination is the human ability to create, receive and communicate images of truth in its diverse forms. It participates in prophetic inspiration, in visionary experiences, in the psalms and wisdom literature of the Old Testament, and in the parabolic teaching ministry of Jesus. The epistles of the New Testament are filled with pictures, images, analogies, and without the imaginative faculty scripture could not be conceived, written or communicated.

Imagination and Scripture

It is quite clear, then, that one brings one's imaginative faculties to the reading of scripture, allowing scripture to stimulate the imagination. In what has been called Primordial Revelation, the Holy Spirit imparts imaginative vision in a prophetic character like Moses. He is minding his father-in-law's sheep in the desert, when suddenly he is confronted with the bush that burned but was not consumed. Or Joseph dreams his dreams of cornfields and celestial bodies which stimulate his imaginative vision of the future. Ezekiel has a vision of a deep, wide river flowing from the throne of God in the temple and carrying life and fertility wherever it goes. Isaiah has a vision of the heavenly court, and is caught up into the glory and wonder of holiness, purgation and prophecy. The book of Daniel is full of imaginative apocalyptic visions of the future, and no little imaginative power is required even to set down the visions, let alone interpret them. In the New Testament, the apocalyptic book *The Revelation to John* calls into play all the powers of the imagination in the portrayal of its visions and in the expectation of the fulfilment of its prophecies.

In all these confrontations, the Holy Spirit is at work, and in my approach to scripture I allow my imaginative and creative faculties to be open to the Spirit's inspiration, so that he who inspired the visions and the writings can also inspire my reading, interpretation and understanding of God's written word to the Church down the ages, and to me, here, today.

In the next section, I shall commend a way of reading and meditating upon scripture so that the Holy Spirit can illuminate the imaginative and creative faculties, but I am not implying that this is the only way to approach scripture – indeed taken alone, it is dangerous. There is a necessary and important place for intellectual study, the learning and interpreting of the Hebrew and Greek text, and the application of the critical faculties, applying the methods of form and critical evaluation. There is also the liturgical reading and expounding of the text in public worship, and the group and personal bible study which is indispensable to the life of the worshipping and serving congregaton and fellowship. The basic academic, literary and theological tools such as scholarly and devotional commentaries are necessary in all this. But I am more concerned in this book with direct confrontation with the text in mediative prayer. This may also be good advice in sermon preparation too, for as William Barclay says in his autobiography: 'I am convinced that the first panic-stricken rush into the arms of the waiting commentators is the death of any originality a man may possess.'

I read scripture critically and intellectually; I read scripture liturgically; I read scripture in preparation for expounding its content in sermon and group study; I read scripture in teaching novices and in other ministries of retreats, lecturing and writing; I read scripture for private devotional and informative puposes. All these 'readings' of scripture are part of my christian privilege and duty. But my meditative reading of scripture is the precious way of entry into prayer in which the Holy Spirit inspires my imaginative faculties so that I am actually drawn into the gospel narratives. I company with Jesus on his preaching journeys, in his teaching, gazing with wonder upon his healing miracles, listening with joy and apprehension when he teaches divine truth.

Sometimes, I become the woman taken in adultery, Zacchaeus the tax-collector up the tree, Nathanael meditating under the fig tree. I am *there*, watching, participating, sharing. I repent with the sinner, am cleansed with the leper or healed with the paralytic. My blind eyes are opened, my deaf ears unstopped, my lame legs begin to dance, my tongue is loosed to sing and praise my Saviour. And then there are times of perplexity and darkness when I climb the mountain with Jesus as the night comes on. I see him fall upon his face before the Father; I see his body tremble and shudder with adoration and longing for the glory which he shared with the Father before the world was made. There are times when I stand afar off, like Peter, and look on in wonder, apprehension and fear, realising how little I know and understand.

Imagination must be Sanctified

Sometimes we are imaginatively present in scripture as observers and sometimes as participants. It depends on the passage of scripture and its teaching and function in our meditation. But it must be emphasised that it is a sanctified and dedicated imagination which is involved. This should be self-evident, but it needs to be stressed. There have been catholic and protestant wars which have taken scripture as their justification, and it is a depraved and carnal imagination that conjures the name of God for the justification of war. Calling a war 'holy' does not make it so, and great danger lies in the fact that an ungodly imagination (or even a 'neutral' imagination) can be stimulated to war and bloodshed by martial music, powerful oratory and the rehearsing of biblical precedents to war.

The bible is well aware of the power of an imagination which is not dedicated to God and the possibilities for evil that are inherent in its unrestrained freedom. Depicting a situation of rebellion against God in Noah's day, we read: 'The Lord saw that the wickedness of man was great in the earth, and that every imagination of the thoughts of his heart was only evil continually.' (Gen. 6:5). The *Magnificat* speaks of God scattering the pround in the imagination of their hearts, and in the *Epistle to the Romans* St Paul speaks of the invisible nature of God being displayed in the natural world, affirming the sanctified use of the imagination, but then goes on to speak of those who have turned their backs upon such a revelation: '. . . although they knew God they did not honour him as God or give thanks to him, but they became futile in their thinking and their senseless minds were darkened.' (Rom. 1:21).

Man is caught up in the dilemma in which his mind is darkened and alienated from the life of God, and the only way out of this impasse is to seek a cleansing, renewal and sanctification of the whole man, involving the mind with all its imaginative powers. For Paul himself makes such an appeal later in the same letter when he calls upon the Roman believers to consecrate themselves, body, mind and spirit to the service of God:

> I appeal to you therefore, brethren, by the mercies of God, to present your bodies as a living sacrifice, holy and acceptable to God, which is your spiritual worship. Do not be conformed to this world, but be transformed by the renewal of your mind, that you may prove what is the will of God, what is good and acceptable and perfect. (Rom. 12:1,2).

The word *transformation (metamorphosis)* in that text is the same as is used for *transfiguration* in the Transfiguration narratives of the synoptic gospels, indicating that it is the same Spirit who renews and sanctifies the disciple and transfigures the Saviour on the holy mountain. The mind of Christ should be within the disciple, with every thought captive to him, and the imagination thus consecrated to his service. It was through the medium of such consecrated imagaination that prophets and apostles could dream and write, could receive vision and revelation, and could portray Christ evidently set forth

27

crucified before their hearers/readers. And it is the same consecrated imagination that receives and communicates the apostolic vision of Christ crucified, risen and coming in glory. The canon of scripture is the repository of vision, and the Holy Spirit inspires the reader, as of old he inspired the writer, so that the truth of the Gospel is rekindled in the believing heart, and proclaimed through the sanctified imagination.

Imaginative Illustration

Before we go on to the actual principles and pratice of meditation, I want to end this section by sharing three illustrations of the way in which the imagination is stimulated by the reading/hearing of scripture which arise from my own experience. The first comes from a simple and direct evangelistic exposition of scripture in preaching. This is especially applicable in the preaching of what I would call the 'story-telling' peoples such as the Celts. In my early christian life it was the Welsh Baptist tradition, but similar experiences are true of the Irish catholic mission preaching of the religious orders. It operates powerfully for me, for I am both Welsh and a Franciscan!

When King George VI died I was about sixteen years of age, and on the Sunday evening I went to Church, and the minister in his thematic and relevant way, announced his text: 'In the year that king Uzziah died, I saw the Lord, sitting upon a throne, high and lifted up . . .' (Isa. 6:1). He was a powerful and imaginative preacher, and he compared and contrasted the earthly and heavenly royal court, the monarch upon his throne and especially the high and sacred mystery of Isaiah's vision of unutterable and ineffable glory. I was at an impressionable age, saw the topical relevance of the text, and listened enthralled, to the story-telling preaching of a man who had been a manual worker in the local steelworks, an amateur athlete and had been ordained later in his forties. He had not had the kind of academic training that led to a divinity degree, but had experienced a powerful evangelical conversion as a young man,

28

and lived in daily confrontation with scripture which gave to his preaching an imaginative and communicative approach, with a sharp, cutting edge which caught up the whole congregation into the world of the bible. That particular occasion was one of many, and he carried us into the mystery and awe of Isaiah's call, cleansing and commissioning, with such power and authority that the sermon remains with me to this day. This therefore provides me with an illustration of the imaginative meditation on scripture by a whole congregation engaged in worship – the preacher leading such meditation. As I say, this is as true of the catholic mission preaching as it is of evangelistic gospel preaching – if the centre is Christ as Lord and Saviour, and the prophetic tradition of the bible is communicated.

My second illustration comes from the particular rough-neck school I attended between the ages of eleven and thirteen, but a school which had some wise and able teachers. One of them taught us, in his own style of religious lessons, many of the prayer book collects and sections of scripture through calligraphy and song. We loved singing, and the roughest and toughest of that exhuberant bunch of forty or so lads looked forward to the way he would communicate intuitively, through his firm but loving personality. There was one particular hymn which we loved, and the meaning of the biblical passage expounded through the words of the hymn was highlighted by the gentle, controlled singing of the verses, and the rip-roaring crescendo of the rising exitement of the refrain, dying down to the last lines of tranquillity and peace. The lads may not have been very literate or philosophically perceptive, but they certainly got the intuitive feel of the passage – they were *there*!

The text of the story of Jesus stilling the tempest on the Lake of Galilee is found in Mark 4:35-41, and is a powerful illustration of the imagination of the gospel writer working on the incident he records. Imagine forty lusty voices, beginning in a controlled manner to get into the feel of the first verse of the hymn in the Sankey tradition:

Master, the tempest is raging!
    The billows are rising high!
The sky is o'ershadowed with blackness,
    No shelter or help is nigh:
Carest thou not that we perish?
    How canst thou lie asleep
When each moment so madly is threatening
    A grave in the angry deep?

The scene is set, the boys are ready, there is a tense
anticipation of excitement and a tingling feeling of sympathetic
shared fear, apprehension, followed by deliverance, victory and
assurance. The voice of Jesus rings out across the angry waves
and roaring wind:

The wind and the waves shall obey my will,
    Peace, be still!
Whether the wrath of the storm-tossed sea,
    Or demons or men or whatever it be,
No waters can swallow the ship where lies
    The Master of ocean and earth and skies.
They all shall sweetly obey my will:
    Peace, be still! Peace, be still!
They all shall sweetly obey my will!
    Peace! Peace! be still!

This a hymn of the evangelistic gospel tradition, with no
pretence of high literary merit (doggerel, some would call it!),
and certainly folksy, perhaps distasteful to certain musical ears,
but the fact was that the scripture story, the rhymed exegesis
and the 'pop' musical approach conveyed and communicated
gospel truth and experience in a way that got at the lives of a
bunch of rough lads with breaking voices – and they enjoyed it!
It was about that time that I had my twelve-year-old
conversion experience, and my appreciation of the hymn was
strengthened by my simple but real experience of trusting

Christ as Saviour. I quote the remaining two stanzas for they make clear the evangelistic import of the hymn in proclaiming Jesus as Master and Saviour, with the expectation of the singer entering into the deliverance experience of the frightened disciples on the storm-tossed lake so long ago:

> Master, with anguish of spirit
>   I bow in my grief today;
> The depths of my sad heart are troubled;
>   Oh waken and save, I pray!
> Torrents of sin and of anguish
>   Sweep o'er my sinking soul;
> And I perish! I perish! dear Master,
>   Oh hasten, and take control.
>
> Master, the terror is over,
>   The elements sweetly rest;
> Earth's sun in the calm lake is mirrored,
>   And heaven's within my breast;
> Linger O blessed Redeemer,
>   Leave me alone no more;
> And with joy I shall make the blest harbour,
>   And rest on the blissful shore.

My third illustration is taken from the evangelistic ministry among young people. From sixteen years of age into my twenties I did a lot of evangelism and counselling among children and teens at seaside services and in various young people's clubs and groups. One evening in my early ministry we organised a barbecue with midnight bathing on Lavernock beach on the South Wales coast. We built a large bonfire on the beach, and after eating greasy hamburgers and running wildly in and out of the water in the moonlight, we eventually settled down in groups around the bonfire, singing to guitars and sharing in the epilogue. The crowd of about fifty or sixty were mainly committed young Christians with invited friends, and without any pressure or pseudo-piety we listened to the reading of St John 21:1-18, a scene set on the shore of Galilee.

You can imagine the scene: a clear moonlit night; groups of friends sitting and lying around the fire on the beach; a light breeze blowing over the sea, and the gentle whispering and breaking of the waves upon the shore. I told the story, communicated imaginatively the scene on the shore of Galilee as the disciples gathered around the fire Jesus had made, and followed the text in the searching of Peter's mind and heart as Jesus called him into the fellowship of forgiveness and love.

There were many such times as this, and it was not only an opportunity for committed young people to share in recreation fellowship, but also for them to bring their friends to a neutral place where the stories of the Gospel could be simply and imaginatively shared. This frequently led to pastoral counselling and prayer singly and in groups, and variations of this practice form the basis of many christian holidays and camps, and this illustration serves to make clear the imaginative use of scripture in that context.

All this illustrative material comes from an immersion in the context and content of scripture, and it is now time that we turned to the actual work of scripture in meditation, for it is only in praying in and through scripture that it can be seen and felt to communicate the power and joy that is inherent in the experiences beneath the surface of the written word, for meditation upon scripture is to be submerged deeper into prayer.

4: Meditation

Deeper Into Prayer

Scripture is meant to proclaim and witness to the saving acts of God in Christ; to be read for proclamation, doctrine, teaching, ethics and wisdom. It is to be used in evangelism and worship, to be read liturgically and privately, meant to be expounded, learned and lived. I have said that there are many tools for proper exegesis that may legitimately be used, but our concern is with the immediate confrontation with the text of scripture for the purposes of meditation and prayer. Meditation implies and necessitates the function of the mind and the use of the imagination, with the disciplined constraint of the facts of the text within the common understanding of the Church.

It is not a matter of turning scripture into sermons, ethical teaching, exhortation, action or holiness. It is a matter of turning scripture into prayer. Meditation is that function of the mind and heart whereby you go beyond the word of scripture and enter into its very heart:

> Break now the bread of life
>   Dear Lord, to me,
> As once you broke the bread
>   Beside the sea;
> Beyond the sacred page
>   I seek you, Lord,
> My spirit longs for you,
>   O living Word.

What Jesus did *then* on the shore of Galilee he does *now* in this place where I covenant to meet with him in prayer and meditation. Scripture becomes the heart of my prayer as the Holy spirit illuminates my mind and enables me to see and touch and taste and possess Christ in his loveliness and fulness – or rather enables me to be possessed by him.

Varieties of Method

A number of 'devotions' have arisen in the practice of the Church which use scripture imaginatively in the context of meditation and prayer. Walking *The Stations of the Cross* is a biblical following on the road to Calvary with Christ which involves the identification of the believer or group with the suffering and death of Jesus. Liturgical devotions such as the washing of feet ceremony dramatically and imaginatively re-enact the incident recorded in John 15:1-15; and the stripping of the altar on Maundy Thursday portrays the forsaking of Jesus by his disciples and the stripping of his garments, while the psalm of dereliction (22) is recited by the people.

There are many devotions of this kind, but the most important are the sacraments of baptism and the eucharist. At the eucharist, to the accompanying words of scripture and prayer, there is enacted the events of the last supper and the death, burial and resurrection of Jesus, with the material elements of bread and wine. In the catholic tradition there may be also the use of incense, water, flame, liturgical colour and ritual gestures of gospel meaning. And in the case of baptism, pouring, or immersion in water.

I have always felt that the Church ecumenical is the poorer for its neglect of the pratice of the baptism of believers by immersion. Both the *Anglican Book of Common Prayer* and the *Alternative Service Book 1980* allows for this 'dipping or pouring', and many missionary priests and bishops practise such baptisms in local rivers. My own (anglo-catholic) parish at home has a baptistery sunk into the floor at the door of the church for the baptism of adults by immersion. The veteran

34

missionary bishop Stephen Neill once spoke at a Baptist Missionary Conference at the Baptist Church in Ruschlikon-Zurich, and surprised us all when he claimed to have baptised more believers by immersion than any Baptist minister present. His claim was, I believe, substantiated!

I mention this because the re-enactment of the sacrament of baptism in a deep baptistery (or better, a river), proclaims the Gospel of the believer's identification with the dying and risen Christ in a unique manner. It not only demonstrates the dying and rising process in an unforgettable and deeply emotional experience, but also involves the congregation in such participation that it becomes a time of worship and meditation, so clearly setting forth the indentification-theology behind Romans 6:3-5.

All these devotional and sacramental practices have spiritual and imaginative value according to the churchmanship of the Christians concerned, but there is a simple method of meditation in which everyone can participate, involving only the opening of the mind and heart to the power of scripture in meditative prayer. This is as open to sacramental Christians as to those (eg Quakers and Salvationists) who have few or no external sacramental signs in their gatherings. It is a method which is as natural to the Christian as a child taking milk from its mother's breast. The trouble with us is that we have forgotten to be like children, and that is why we fall short of true conversion. There is a beautiful imaginative picture of the believer meditating upon the word and will of God in Psalm 131:

> I have calmed and quieted my soul,
> Like a child quieted at its mother's breast;
> Like a child that is quiet is my soul.

Another picture of the meditative soul is that of a cow lying in the shade of a meadow tree, quietly ruminating and chewing her cud in tranquillity and gentleness. But these are analogies, and the application may not be so easy, for after all, we are not infants at our mother's breast, or bovine creatures lying in the shade of a spreading chestnut tree, while the rest of the world goes by! So we must talk about *how* to do it, but before we go into the actual mechanics of meditation we must turn our attention to the content of scripture, which is, after all, the rock from which we quarry the materials for our meditative work. When St Paul wrote to Timothy, he reminded him not to be a disputer of words involving himself in unprofitable chatter: 'Do your best to present yourself to God as one approved, a workman who has no need to be ashamed, rightly handling the word of truth.'

Illustrative Old Testament Passages

The word *inspiration* immediately calls to mind the breathing of God's Holy Spirit of life, illumination and wisdom into the inanimate body of Adam in the Genesis creation story. It is the breath that inspires life in every created being, and breathes through the whole created order. When Jesus breathed on his disciples after the resurrection it was in anticipation of the coming of the Holy Spirit. And this is the same Spirit who inspired the biblical prophets and writers, and who inspires those who, with believing hearts and enlightened minds, come to scripture for guidance and sustenance – though he may blaze out in warning and judgment!

The stimulation of a purified and enlightened imagination is the prerequisite for revelation and inspiration, and scripture yields its abundance to those who are thus prepared. The canon of scripture is a treasure-house from which truths are learned; it is the hidden treasure in the field which must be sought by digging deeply; it is the market-place filled with precious pearls and the most perfect pearl is the Christ. From a child I have been aware of the power of scripture to move me to laughter and tears, firing my imagination and energising my will. I have been in the garden of Eden both in innocence and guilt, and have witnessed the expulsion from the garden into a wandering life of sorrow and alienation. I have wandered in the wilderness with Jacob and dreamed with him of the ladder stretching to heaven with angels ascending and descending, and I have trembled with him as the angel-figure laid hold on him in the dark hours of the night and wrestled with him until break of day. I have found myself in Joseph's skin as he basked in his father's favour, became hated and betrayed by his brothers, was cast into the pit, rose in Potipher's household, was flung into prison under a false charge and rose to the Pharaoh's right hand by the providential power of God. I watched with Miriam as baby Moses was hidden in the bullrushes, was adopted and grew up in the court of Pharaoh, slew an Egyptian, fled into the desert and met the Hebrew God in the burning bush. I travelled through the wilderness all those long and weary years under the charismatic leadership of Moses and Aaron; was scorched with the ineffable glory and holiness of God on Mount Sinai, wept at the idolatory of the children of Israel, and came at last to the promised land of milk and honey under Joshua.

I have wondered at the incredible escapades of the Judges, and romanticised over the lovely book of Ruth. The call of Samuel has always held me spellbound, and the amazing cycle of David stories has caused in me admiration, disgust, loathing, incredulity and wonder at the amazing grace of God operative in a man of such heights and depths of spirituality and carnality. The Elijah cycle of stories with sustaining ravens, fire from heaven and desert spirituality has fired and sustained me, and I have trailed behind Elisha dipping in the Jordan with Namaan for healing of leprosy, and breathless with fear and excitement as the enemies of the Lord surrounded us, while hosts of the heavenly beings circled above us.

The prophetic call stories of Isaiah, Jeremiah and Ezekiel provoke intense reaction within me, with mingled awe and fear, while Ezekiel in his valley of dry bones, or up to his chin in the divine river makes me yearn for ever-deepening experiences of God. Small books like Esther and Jonah surround me with the protection and grace of God, and the sheer beauty and loveliness of the carnal and spiritual love of the Song of Solomon stirs up longings for the eternal love within my heart. All these aspects of Old Testament revelation, with their warnings and judgments, mirror my own spiritual experience, and together with the wisdom tradition and the call to purity and holiness I find my life enriched and challenged to an ever-closer confrontation with the God who is at the heart of the Old Testament revelation. Jesus' roots were Jewish, earthy, imaginative, not philosophically speculative but rooted in the soil of human experience, so that Old Testament experience becomes *my* experience and Jesus' forefathers become *my* patriarchs, seers, prophets and guides.

The Flowering of the New Testament

The prophetic imagination of the Old Testament is fulfilled in the person of Jesus. He is the Messiah, Suffering Servant, the prophet foreshadowed by Moses, the Priest foreshadowed by Aaron and Melchisedek and the King foreshadowed by David. Law, prophets and psalms bear abundant witness to his coming, and the New Testament overflows with messianic joy. The gospels reveal him, the epistles proclaim him, the New Testament Church experiences him and the apocalypse expects him in power and great glory, ushering in the consummation of all things, when God the Father shall be all in all.

Companying with Jesus

The sum and centre of New Testament teaching is not that we follow *after* Jesus as an example, though, of course, that is involved. Neither is it that we walk *beside* Jesus as Saviour, Friend and Brother, though these aspects of discipleship and learning are part of the whole story. Nor is it that we *respond* to Jesus as servant to Lord, though obedience is an integral part of response to his love. But the wonderful mystery of the Gospel is that Jesus the Christ *dwells within us*. The indwelling Christ is the basis of the assurance of forgiveness, the mainspring of holiness and the dynamic of christian living. It is in meditation upon the word of scripture that such an understanding becomes a vital and indispensable experience of spiritual life. Take the words of Jesus in the seventh chapter of St John:

If any one thirst, let him come to me and drink. He who believes in me, as the scripture has said, out of his heart (lit. innermost being) shall flow rivers of living water.

John makes the point that Jesus was referring to the *indwelling Spirit* that would come upon the disciples, for there is a kind of interchangeability between the persons of Jesus and the Spirit indwelling the believer in the New Testament. The indwelling Spirit within bears witness to the Jesus who meets us in scripture. The bible is an objective check upon our interior imagination. The constraint and discipline of the sacred texts keep us in the way of truth, so that we do not remake Jesus in our own image. It is the Jesus of the bible, the Jesus of the Church that we seek, and the meditating believer prays:

Let the beauty of Jesus be seen in me,
All his wondrous compassion and purity;
O thou Spirit divine, all my nature refine,
Till the beauty of Jesus is seen in me.

We walk with Jesus through the pages of the New Testament, watching, observing, participating in the incidents recorded, and we are drawn into the text, and feel the light and the darkness, the healing and the pain, the heights and the depths which meet us in the gospels. There will be times when we shall sit in wonder with the crowds on the hill of the beatitudes; we shall look upon Jesus as he lays his healing hands upon the loathsome leper, casts out evil spirits and gives sight to the blind. There will be times when we shall climb the mountain of transfiguration and become bewildered by his glory or shiver with awe and trembling with the disciples in the boat as he moves across the surface of the waters of Galilee in the early morning. There will be moments of great gladness as we hear the hosannas of the people, followed by times of increasing darkness and sorrow, as with Peter, James and John we huddle in Gethsemane, while Jesus, a stone's throw away, is stretched on the ground, pleading with his Father through the sweat and blood of Gethsemane.

Along the way of sorrows we shall follow him to the hill called Calvary, and shudder as he is stretched upon the cross, hanging between earth and heaven for the sins of the world. Then there will be the waiting, watching and hoping through the dark hours in the garden of the tomb where he is buried. We shall feel the quivering of anticipation in the air, the stirring of the Spirit's life within the tomb, and the burst and blaze of divine glory as he shatters the bronze gates of hell, breaking the chains of death, rolling the stone away and emerging triumphantly in the glory of immortal life. All this, and more, is possible as we give ourselves to meditation in the pages of the gospels, and as we company with the earthly and glorified Jesus.

Setting About It

If our minds and hearts have been touched and moved by the need and longing for prayer and meditation, then we shall require some plain and practical explanation of how to set about it. It is quite clear that prayer is both an inspired movement within the heart and also a discipline to be integrated into the wholeness of one's daily life. If there is no fire then there will be no light or heat, and if there is no discipline then the ignited coals will soon burn themselves out. But presuming that there is a kindling flame on the altar of the heart – how does one tend it, nurture it, sustain it? I am concerned with a particular kind of meditation, that which feeds upon scripture and draws from it the initial ignition by the Holy Spirit and the sustaining fuel that keeps it burning. The

40

Holy Spirit is the igniting power and the text of scripture is the fuel – but it must burn upon the altar of my heart – and the *heart* in this context is the wholeness of my imaginative being, the surrender of my mind to God with all its logical and intuitive processes. This kind of meditation takes place within the body, for we are not discarnate spirits, but incarnate beings.

There are five steps to meditation which are simple to uncomplicated people, but need both fire and perseverence to those of us who have substituted complexity for our early simplicty. They are:

1 Relaxation
2 Respiration
3 Visualisation
4 Participation
5 Adoration

The first step, *Relaxation* refers to the body and the mind. It means that in stillness of body and mind is the preparation for prayer. The second step, *Respiration* has to do with the Holy Spirit and the human spirit. The word *spiration* means *breath*, and the Holy Spirit is the breath of God, so that *inspiration* is the human spirit being breathed into by the Holy Spirit. The third step, *Visualisation* is the consequence of such inspiration – it is the enlightenment of the imagination and the heart as you focus upon the text of scripture before you, so that it can yield up its hidden treasure. *Participation* is the fourth step in which you are taken up and into scripture actually experiencing the biblical incident, or being carried into the context of the passage. The work of meditation is then well under way, and the fifth step, *Adoration* indicates the mind and heart set upon God, and this fifth step opens up a deeper level of understanding and experience which borders on vision and contemplation. Let us take the steps progressively.

1 Relaxation
Meditation is a work as well as an art, and setting about it

41

requires first of all, a place. It needs to be secluded, quiet and conducive to prayer. Of course one can pray anywhere and at any time, and there are situations in which prayer is called for in crowded, dangerous or unusual situations, or when the Lord just 'takes over' without warning. But here we are concerned with the work of meditation on a regular and disciplined basis. The place may be the corner of a church, an oratory, a quiet room, a hut in the garden, an open field in the country, or some bolt-hole where you can get away from disturbance. It is best to avoid tight clothing; a track/leisure suit is best, and no footgear.

Then you need to apply the principle of relaxation to your body. It means first finding the right posture – which may be sitting on a stool or upright chair, kneeling with the aid of a prayer-stool, sitting in a cross-legged/lotus posture, or lying upon the ground on back or tummy (the latter may be too soporific for some people). My chosen posture is the prayer-stool kneeling position.

Then the simple process of relaxation can be practised. This can be found in any relaxation literature, and basically it means beginning with the soles of the feet and progressing up to the crown of the head, stretching and relaxing, telling each part of your body to let go, and rest. It is worth getting some advice, and doing some relaxation exercises with a group or with someone who knows it well. When the body is relaxed but alert, and the back is straight, then attention must be given to breathing, which brings us to the second step.

2 Respiration
The second step is the opening of the human spirit to the Holy Spirit. You give attention to your breathing – your own respiration, and to the breathing of the Spirit of God who dwells within you. In terms of respiration, it is a good practice to learn to breathe from the diaphragm rather than from the top of the chest – belly breathing instead of shallow chest breathing. Slow, deep, rhythmic breathing – but with no push or strain. Everything should be easy – easy come, easy go.

Continue breathing like this for a minute or two until you find your own gentle rhythm. At this point, people who practise the *Jesus Prayer* either begin to say the prayer according to their breathing rhythm, or they become aware of the heart-beat and repeat the prayer according to that measure. This is the point at which we look to the Lord to guide us in prayer, for inspiration is also the saying of the prayer: 'Breathe on me, Breath of God.' True prayer is the human spirit experiencing the indwelling and guidance of the divine Spirit ever deeper into the divine Love.

3 Visualisation

There are many forms of imaginative prayer, dream and vision, both inside and outside the biblical pages. Our concern is with the stimulation of the imaginative vision by the word of scripture. If we have opened our minds and hearts to the inspiration of the Holy Spirit and we have the word of scripture before us, then we shall be guided by the text into a meditative understanding. We shall be carried into scripture's plain meaning, into the implications of its teaching and into a personal or group application of its meaning for our day, for our lives, for our present situation.

Care must be exercised in such practice, especially if we are tempted to allegorical or mystical interpretations which bear no relation to its plain and obvious meaning. We must remain, on fundamentals, within the certain consensus of opinion within the Church's doctrine. But of course, there are many applications of scripture which may be of value from a psychological and personal viewpoint, which do not indulge in fanciful or heretical doctrinal opinions. Within scripture itself, we see that the imagination is stimulated often by dreams in which God gives guidance or prophecy (eg Joseph of Genesis and Joseph of the gospels), and by presentiments, prophecies and visions given to groups and individuals who communicate teaching to the Church of God (eg Agabus' prophecy by the Spirit, of the famine in Acts 11:27-30). Such gifts remain in the Church and were not meant only for the apostolic period, but they must be subject to the teaching of scripture and of the mainstream tradition of the Church. Visualisation then is the opening up and stimulation of the imagination by the Holy Spirit before the written text of scripture.

4 Participation

The fourth step in our meditative process is when the believer is carried into the pages of the bible, actually participating in the situation described in the text. You begin by an objective evaluation of the scene, and then allow yourself to be ever more deeply drawn into the activity and movement of the story, parable, miracle or whatever passage is being studied. This is an imaginative participation by experience, so that you identify with Abraham being called out from Ur of the Chaldees, Isaac walking to sacrifice with his father up Mount Moriah, Jacob running away in the wilderness from Esau, Samuel the child as he hears God calling to him in the darkness, or with Jeremiah or the psalmist lying in a well or pit of despair. In the New Testament the gospels and the Acts of the Apostles are full of situations which may become relevant to your own pilgrimage and vocation. As well as giving clear ethical and doctrinal teaching, they are full of situations and principles of action which impinge on our own corporate and personal lives.

We make scripture our own by such imaginative and prayerful participation in its pages, so that the characters of the bible become our friends, and their lives intertwine with ours in the pilgrimage of faith. When St Paul spoke of the journey of the children of Israel in the wilderness he clearly meant that their journey should become ours, and that we should identify with their pilgrimage in the avoiding of sins and the following of our heavenly Moses in the journey from earth to heaven (eg 1 Cor. 10:1-13). The writer of the Hebrew letter certainly meant us to identify with the heroes of faith so that we may enter into their experience and emulate their faith and victory (see Heb. ch. 11 *passim*), and he concludes:

> Therefore, since we are surrounded by so great a cloud of witnesses, let us also lay aside every weight and sin which clings so closely, and let us run with perseverance the race that is set before us, looking to Jesus the pioneer and perfecter of our faith . . .

Ultimately, it is participation *with* Jesus in the words and works of his ministry on earth, and participation and identification *in* Jesus as he enters into the pain and sorrows of Calvary and death and rises into glory and newness of life. Such identification is the root and sap of christian mystical theology, exemplified by St Paul in words which would be amazing if they were not so familiar:

> I have been crucified with Christ; it is no longer I who live, but Christ who lives in me; and the life I now live in the flesh I live by faith in the Son of God, who loved me and gave himself for me.
> (Gal. 2:20)

5 *Adoration*

I mean by the use of this word to include a wide spectrum of experience and attitude, from a simple sense of wonder at the beauty and power of Jesus speaking, healing, dying and rising in the pages of the gospels to the timeless contemplative adoration of eternal union with God which is beyond language and understanding to us in this life. It is the endless, adoring wonder of those who are caught up into the very being of God in his eternal, trinitarian life of glory and love – the consummation of all things in which rests the stillness and the dynamic of all creation.

We must leave aside the eternal dimension for the present, because that belongs rather to contemplation than to meditation. But if we embark upon the meditative reading and praying of scripture we shall certainly glimpse something of the eternal glory of God in Jesus, by the power of the Holy Spirit. If we company with the seers, prophets, apostles and with Jesus himself, we shall be struck down with the wonder and majesty of God, we shall be melted by his love and transfigured by his glory. Isaiah cried out in mortal and spiritual agony at the vision of God; Ezekiel fell on his face before God's glory, and Daniel felt all the strength drain away before the vision. At one point Peter looked upon the face of Jesus and said: 'Depart from me, for I am a sinful man, O Lord.' And when the three disciples entered into the cloud of glory on Tabor, they became speechless with adoring wonder.

I have been consciously following the way of Jesus since I

was twelve years of age, (and unconsciously ever since I can remember), and some of the most precious and revelatory moments of my life have been the experiences of God within the pages of holy scripture. I understand very well why Antony the hermit was smitten by scripture in the third century, sold all his possessions and followed Christ into the desert; why Augustine, hearing the word of God in the garden in Milan in the fourth century suddenly gave up his immoral and restless life, surrendering to God in conversion; why Francis of Assisi, hearing the word of the Gospel in the thirteenth centry embraced poverty, celibacy and obedience to live a simple gospel life with his brothers. It was the result of a meditative listening to the word of scripture while the inspiring spirit moved within their hearts.

I have laughed and I have wept; I have danced and I have lain smitten on the ground; I have proclaimed with great assurance and been struck to silence – all because of the power of the Holy Spirit within my heart through the word of scripture. And I can translate that last sentence quite easily into the present tense, for it happens now – it happens today, as I hear and understand, and give my mind and heart to obedience and love. Adoration is the word which covers the whole spectrum of response, for out of the experience of adoring wonder, there is the overflow of a life given to God in words and works of love. The first commandment is to love God with all the heart and soul and mind and strength, and the overflow of such adoring love is the love of neighbour – including friend and enemy – in the reconciling Gospel of Jesus. As an aid to memory, then, I set out the five steps again in relation to their meaning:

1. Relaxation (of the body)
2. Respiration (in the Spirit)
3. Visualisation (through the scriptures)
4. Participation (with Christ)
5. Adoration (of God)

Letting It Happen

Now, in the spirit of simplicity, openness and expectation, and following the pattern just described, I shall allow the Lord to take me deeper into himself by the power of the Spirit at work in scripture. I take the Gospel of St Mark 5: verses 24-34 – the healing of the woman with the chronic haemorrhage.

A great crowd followed Jesus and thronged about him. And there was a woman who had had a flow of blood for twelve years, and who had suffered much under many physicians, and had spent all that she had, and was no better but rather grew worse.

She had heard the reports about Jesus, and came up behind him in the crowd and touched his garment. For she said, 'If I touch even his garments, I shall be made well.'

And immediately, the haemorrhage ceased; and she felt in her body that she was healed of her disease.

And Jesus, perceiving in himself that power had gone forth from him, immediately turned about in the crowd, and said, 'Who touched my garments?' And his disciples said to him, 'You see the crowd pressing around you, and yet you say, "Who touched me?" ' And he looked around to see who had done it.

But the woman, knowing what had been done to her, came in fear and trembling and fell down before him, and told him the whole truth. And he said to her, 'Daughter, your faith has made you well; go in peace, and be healed of your disease.'

First of all I find a quiet place, a small room set apart for meditation, with an icon and a candle burning before it. I wear loose clothing with no footgear. I sit on my prayer-stool, with straight back and no strain, allowing any stress and 'up-tightness' to flow away in the relaxing atmosphere of the loving presence of God. I allow a minute or two to settle down, then gently begin to practise the relaxation technique of stretching and relaxing from the soles of my feet to the crown of my head. Then gently, I allow my breathing to slow down and deepen – belly-breathing instead of shallow chest-breathing. I become aware of the Holy Spirit, the breath of God, breathing in and through me.

Now, when I find myself outwardly and inwardly quiet, I take up the text and read it right through, not hurriedly, but not yet dwelling on any particular words or phrases, in order to set the scene and be surrounded by the context of the story.

So I arrive at the place where I read the text again – but this time slowly and imaginatively, waiting, watching, enquiring – moving from one part of the scene to another, or quietly observing various characters in their interaction and movement. Sometimes this is the most fruitful part of the meditation because the words and phrases allow my participation as I move through the text sequentially. But at other times I let the text minister to me, closing my eyes and allowing the story to unfold in imaginative vision, and am borne along in the meditation by the Spirit's interior movement.

On this occasion, I find myself carried into the text as I read it, and feel it drawing out of me my own feelings of curiosity, perplexity, emptiness, weariness, hope, anticipation and growing wonder and faith in Jesus the healer.

The Meditation

I find myself gently being let down into the midst of a great crowd. I am unnoticed because in the shove and push of the crowd we are all trying to move along with Jesus who is on his way to lay hands on a dying girl, daughter of Jairus an elder of the synagogue.

It's a hot day and I can feel the dust between the toes of my sandalled feet – I can hear and see and even smell the crowd thronging and moving along. I'm looking for someone, and at last I see her. I know a bit about her from the text, and as I

48

watch her unobserved, I can see and then feel all her pain and desperation. As I try to enter into the depths of her feelings and understand her longings, I begin to feel myself thinking through her mind, feeling from her heart, longing with her faith.

How long it has been – fully twelve years of weariness and pain, of chronic bleeding, of religious and social rejection. The nature of her disease means that she cannot worship with the people of God and cannot mix freely with any social group. All the money she possessed has long ago been spent on physicians and medicines – all to no avail. She has come to the end of her tether.

Now I can feel the debilitating anxiety, the fear and trembling that takes hold of her as she is moved by the crowd, edging forward toward Jesus. 'If only I can touch him', is the dominant thought in her mind. There is nothing else to do now, nowhere else to go, no-one else to trust – only him. If only . . . All the weariness of twelve long years of sickness and pain, of loneliness and isolation, of fears and rejection, are gathered up in her determination, and all the longing, the hope, the mingled faith and desire which Jesus draws out of her.

Now see her within a stone's throw of him . . . edging, pushing, elbowing nearer. And then, suddenly . . . reaching out . . . touching . . . believing . . . and suddenly – suddenly being shot through with energy strength, power and healing!

> Alleluia!
> It's done!
> In a moment!
> *   WHOLENESS   *
> Alleluia!

The whole world has changed – radiance, healing, physical well-being – and joy! In that one, glorious moment it seems as if the world stands still, the crowd is silenced – there is only JESUS – and her! Alleluia!

And then. A word from heaven. 'Who touched me?' Jesus is

looking around – of course he knows, for as she felt power *enter into her*, he felt power *leaving him*. And she knows. And she knows that he knows, and he knows that she knows! There's no-one else in the world – but she trembles now with a new fear – and yet also vibrant with faith.

Listen to the disciples, irritated and perplexed under the afternoon sun. 'Lord,' says Peter, 'everyone is touching you, look at the crowd – what do you mean?' But she knows, and she comes, and falls down before him, and tells her story – and out it all comes. She tells of the years of pain and weariness, the longing, the uncleanness, the social rejection, the religious isolation, the sheer emptiness of her soul. Her tears are a mingling of sorrow and joy now, and her sadness mingles with his compassion, and again there is no-one else in the world, but Jesus only . . . 'My daughter,' he says, (and his words are like the sound of many waters), 'your faith has made you whole. Go in peace and be free from all your suffering . . .' And the world turns over in love.

These are my tears – this is my joy – and so it all comes back to me. I need you now, Lord. I feel the compassion and healing power flowing through you, and I feel my own bankruptcy and weariness. I am carried deeper and deeper into the healing power of Jesus, by the life-giving dynamism of the Spirit, down into the mystery of the love of God. And on . . . on to adoration . . .

Reflection

At this point I would like the believer to 'take off' under the guidance of the Holy Spirit. That is what scripture mediation is all about. On the one hand I feel I should not give any more direction, but on the other, I am aware that Christians do not spend time with God before scripture in meditative prayer. They read, study, use commentaries, debate and argue, but they do not spend time in meditation, reflection, adoration in the loving presence of God with the text before their eyes and within their hearts. So I shall give some indication of where such meditation may lead you, and the kind of questions which you may ask of the Lord through the text, expecting you to leave all this behind you as you progress in meditative prayer. The following points have our particular miracle-story in mind, but the principles may be adapted to any piece of scripture:

1 Do I identify with any particular person or group within this story? At what points do I see similarities between their situation and mine?

2 If Jesus is the same yesterday, today and forever, do I believe that his words, his direction, his power are directly pointed at me today?

3 Is there a clear word of commitment/direction for me here? Am I led to repentance, deeper faith and trust, a radical change of attitude because of my confrontation with God in this text?

4 Look at the identification-character again, and her suffering, faith and healing. Have I taken time truly to empathise with her helpless need, without rushing on to the happy ending? Her twelve years of suffering deserve twelve minutes of my reflection.

5 Reflection on her suffering raises wider questions of human suffering. What if God allows me to suffer in like manner in the future? I am no better than this woman. God does not *send* suffering, but he does *allow* it. I desperately need the Holy Spirit's guidance, instruction and help at this point.

6 Perhaps here I glimpse the purpose of the gospel-writer. He intends to show progression from suffering through faith to healing in this story. I can only make such a journey if I begin where the woman began, and set my heart upon Jesus as she did.

7 Is it really true that Jesus can direct his healing power into my body and spirit as truly as if I were that woman? And will he do it? And do I have such faith?

8 I come to see that it is not a matter of imagination, but of living faith. I can evoke the images of this text, but I cannot call up or manipulate the power of Jesus. This is what the text is telling me. She directed her whole self to HIM. Only the

Spirit within can cause me to look to the Jesus above. Between the text of scripture and the Spirit's indwelling, there it is that the relation is made real – there it is that the power flows – there it is that God's work is accomplished.

9 What about the other characters in the story? Can I feel for them – see their point of view – identify with their perplexity, their enthusiasm, their alienation, their opposition, or whatever attitude or emotion is expressed by them? Would I prefer to hide in the crowd? Have I ever been truly alone with Jesus – am I ready for it now?

10 Now Jesus himself. Can I see through his eyes, think through his mind, feel through his heart in this story? Now, Lord Jesus, help me to live your experience; to see, feel and touch the world of suffering and need. Especially in the life of this woman. I will be still and let you lead me through the story again – but this time let me experience it all in you.

11 Is this the time to begin to write my impressions? I sense the rightness of the moment, and ask if the Lord has more to show me first . . .
   Yes. I can begin to write my reflections, being open to all that has taken place between the text and myself. I write freely, remaining open to new insights, suggestions and courses of action.

12 My resolution. What is there that I should *do* as a result of my meditation? Is there a change of attitude to put into effect? An apology to be made? Wrong relationships to put right? Money to be returned or donated? Am I called to be a channel of healing in my job, my neighbourhood, school, hospital? Am I to befriend a stranger? Open my home? Try to understand a minority group? Overcome emotional or irrational prejudices? Let me realise that if I have been led along these lines and refuse to act, then my prayer-life will die, and my faith will be vain.

Although the above questions are personal, they can be shared if the context is group meditation. In a plenary session it would be helpful if doubts, fears and frustrations were expressed, rather than give the impression that this kind of meditation is easy, fulfilling and productive for everyone.

The following kinds of responses may be heard: 'I cannot get into this at all – my imagination doesn't work with images.' 'I was alright until I was alone with the woman before Jesus – then I got blocked and could go no further.' 'The scene terrified me. I'd never realised that Jesus acted like this, and he made me afraid.' 'I could feel Jesus telling me that I had never been honest with him or myself before. I couldn't respond immediately, but now something new has begun.' 'For the first time in my life I felt loved. He loved me – he loves me. I began to cry, and now I'm embarrassed, but it's wonderful.' 'I just can't do with this kind of subjective stuff – in fact I think it's dangerous – I really don't think this way of praying is for me.' 'I'm sorry but I don't feel part of this group – but I also feel that the fault is mine.'

Praying the bible in this mediative way opens up entirely new ways of using scripture in prayer. It is rather like the river of God in Ezekiel chapter 47 – there are waters to touch, waters to paddle in, waters to wade in and waters in which to swim. It will become clear that this book is only a suggestive aid. You will need a counsellor, a group and further guidance for the longer pilgrimage.

Length of time given to such meditation will vary greatly depending upon personal temperament, experience of such praying, group-time available. Some will feel antagonistic about it, even threatened by it. This may indicate either that this kind of meditation is premature in the experience of the person, or that gentle experiment should continue alone and with a few friends. It is by co-operation with the Holy Spirit that this way of praying and meditating grows. Remember, it is no new-fangled technique, but ancient meditation!

If you meditate in a group, then you can choose a leader, a narrator, and if some kind of soul-friendship is practised between members of the group there can be a profound personal/corporate sharing.

Also, if you progress in this way of prayer, you may find

yourself crying or laughing, singing or dancing – or what is more likely, you may find yourself prostrate on the ground for long periods of time – perhaps taken out of yourself, and moving into more contemplative dimensions of prayer.

5: Contemplation

The Spirit in Control

It is not the purpose of this small book to deal with the deeper reaches of prayer or mystical theology, but it is necessary to indicate the dimension of prayer that has been called *contemplative*. It used to be thought that contemplative prayer was reserved for mystics and spiritual giants, while the lower plains of meditation were the best that could be hoped for in the experience of ordinary Christians. The New Testament does, certainly, acknowledge that there are spiritual infants and spiritually mature Christians (1 Cor. 3:1-17), but the way is open to all. The Lord could well seize a schoolboy cycling along a country lane, a woman suckling her baby at her breast or a Karl Barth playing an hour of Mozart before working on his *Church Dogmatics*! What I have already written indicates that it is not so much that there are successive and distinct steps, phases or dimensions of prayer, but that there is a gradual ascent, moving from a simple apprehension of God's presence, right up into what has been called the vision of God or loving union – an increasingly profound experience which is itself infinitely progressive.

Nevertheless, it is useful to speak of an area or dimension of prayer which may be called contemplative, for it indicates that the initiator and sustainer of such prayer is the Holy Spirit himself. We are never completely passive, for we consciously (and then unconsciously) co-operate with the Holy Spirit, give ourselves to him, yield our loving obedience trust and dependence, but he is the initiator and ground of our yearning. The word *contemplation* (theoria) includes both thinking and gazing. It is not cerebral, intellectual, academic and discursive thinking, but rather intuitive, visionary and receptive vision. It is where the prayer of meditation is brought into a quietness and calm which leads to adoration and a certain passivity of worship. F.W. Faber catches a glimpse of it in the last stanza of his hymn *My God How Wonderful Thou Art*:

> Father of Jesus, love's reward,
> What rapture will it be
> Prostrate before thy throne to lie
> And gaze, and gaze on thee.

This is the visionary passivity and openness which is receptive of revelation. It is the receptive vessel waiting to be filled with wisdom and perception. And it is brought about by the transforming power of the Holy Spirit.

Of course, it is not everyone's experience that meditative prayer leads on to contemplation. Perhaps few Christians actually do progress in this way. And for others, the progress is not easy from one to the other, for times of conflict, dryness and aridity may intervene, and the impossibility of praying in any imaginative or meditative manner. St John of the Cross is the guide here, and it is outside our immediate area, but I am indicating these things for those who are called into a contemplative way that will demand time and energy at all levels which most of us are unable to give in our present state.

The way is open to all in the sense that all will eventually attain to the fulness of the vision of God. But for most of us the journey will continue after our physical death. What we have to do now is to get into the way of biblical praying, into the practice of basic bible meditation and loving awareness of God which leads to the beginnings of the contemplative way. The basic way of meditation and the deeper contemplative path both have their roots in scripture, and in all parts of the Church. Even if we are beginners in the way (and most of us remain so), we should, at least, be *aware* of the deeper reaches of prayer, for we shall all traverse that way on our ultimate pilgrimage to God.

The Vocation to Contemplative Prayer

I want to sound a warning at this point. It is that both in the charismatic movement and in the new contemplative awareness in the Church, there are certain people who want to be 'in on the act', and they are not always mentally mature. Simon Magus was a false disciple (Acts 8:14-24). He wanted to manipulate the charisms of the Holy Spirit for his own ends. He wanted spiritual power, authority, gifts of grace as if they were magical charms which could be earned or purchased. Not every Christian will be a prophet, a priest, a healer – not every Christian will have the gift of preaching, healing, discernment, tongues or interpretation. And not every Christian will have a particular *vocation* to contemplative prayer. It depends on the distribution of the Holy Spirit (I Cor. 12:4-11), and we cannot push ourselves into ministries which are not for us. There is a kind of contemplative prayer which is the particular calling of those who feel the Spirit moving them in that direction. It has little to do with clerical status, theological education or academic prowess. It has to do with the calling and election of God.

Some are called particularly to preaching, teaching, healing, interpretation, discernment – and some are called to the deeper dimensions of prayer. That is not to say that all Christians are not called to these things *in a measure*. But there are areas and dimensions of contemplative prayer that are dangerous for those who are not called and prepared by the Spirit for such a vocation. There are areas of spiritual conflict, dark powers and psychic danger, which demand not only a definite call from God, but also a sane and balanced mind, and even a sturdy physical constitution, though bearing in mind that God's strength is made perfect in human weakness.

I sound this warning because I meet perplexed people who are trying to run before God, who desire and covet particular gifts that he does not intend to give them, and it amounts to spiritual avarice and coveteousness to go on demanding that

57

which is not for you. Your life is precious to God, and his gifts are for your good and the good of the Church. No-one can take your place in his plan, but then you must not try to usurp another's place because of your own inordinate spiritual desires. This is a hard lesson to learn, but learn it we must, and the consequence of such a lesson well learned is a great sense of relief, contentment and the humility to follow in the way that God wants us to go.

But I can immediately hear the question 'How can I know?' It is not enough to feel a powerful and insistent interior voice, for such things can arise from one's own natural unconscious, or even from dark powers. It is necessary to have any such private call checked by scripture and the wider, discerning body of the Church. 'Beloved, do not believe every spirit,' says St John, 'but test the spirits to see whether they are of God.' (I John 4:1). Such a call, and the discerning tests to be applied, are outside the scope of this book, but this warning and encouragement is necessary.

Spiritual Depth

If you have followed thus far, and put into practice the method of praying the bible, you will already have begun a spiritual exploration that will convince you that there is always more of God to explore, understand and experience, at all levels of your being. Origen, one of the eastern theologians of the early church said that there was a body, a soul and a spirit in scripture. He understood the body as the simple, historical and contextual meaning; the soul as its inner teaching/meaning, such as the parables of Jesus which have to be interpreted; and the spirit is the deep symbolical, allegorical, hidden or mystical meaning, such as the hidden language of the *Apocalypse*, the symbolic and type-teaching of the *Epistle to the Hebrews* and the mystical meaning of books like the *Song of Solomon*, many of the *psalms* and much of the deep teaching on prayer and participation in the life of God.

As we explore these different levels of scripture and prayer we shall take heed of the safeguards of orthodox teaching within the fellowship of the Church, and not go off into private interpretations which lead to sect-like and schismatic groupings. But we shall become aware that our pilgrimage is one which is open to ever-deepening exploration and adventure into God. In this way our lives will be continually transformed and our love and understanding will overflow to influence the lives of others. And this brings me to the last thing I want to mention in relation to the prayerful study of scripture.

6: Communication

The Overflowing Gospel Life

It is certain that a deep life of prayer overflows into a life-style of gospel compassion, though there may be great shyness in sharing it, not because the Christian is ashamed of it but because the experience is too precious to be hawked around. It is almost as if the great gift suffers by speaking about it, and yet there is an immense longing to communicate with those who understand. In *Seeds of Contemplation*, Thomas Merton puts it this way:

> No one is more shy than a contemplative about his contemplation. Sometimes it gives him almost physical pain to speak to anyone of what he has seen of God . . . At the same time he most earnestly wants everybody else to share his peace and joy. His contemplation gives him a new outlook on the world of men. He looks about him with a secret and tranquil surmise which he perhaps admits to no one, hoping to find in the faces of other men or to hear in their voices some sign of vocation and potentiality for the same deep happiness and wisdom.
>
> He finds himself speaking of God to the men in whom he hopes he has recognized the light of his own peace, the awakening of his own secret: or if he cannot speak to them, he writes for them, and his contemplative life is still imperfect without sharing, without companionship, without communion.

In any case, contemplation cannot be taught, and the witness that is to be given is not one which deals with the steps, levels or phases of prayer, but a simple gospel life. I have been recommending an evangelical attention to scripture and a catholic meditative attitude in one's approach. If time and space is given to both these things, then the Holy Spirit will do the rest. The overflow will consist in joy and love. Joy indicates zeal and enthusiasm, and love indicates compassion and sharing. It is not always easy to be both enthusiastic and compassionate, for the wrong kind of zealous enthusiasm can lead to sterile dogmatism and exclusivism. And a sentimental kind of compassion can lead to a watering down of gospel values and a relativising of the demands of Jesus. But a prayerful and contemplative meditation of the scriptures along the lines we have been following will lead to a life so full of the Holy Spirit that joy and compasson will spill over and communicate themselves to those around.

I say 'spill over and communicate' because there will be no need for us to go forcing the Gospel down the throats of recalcitrant unbelievers! If the Gospel does not radiate from our lives, then no amount of verbiage will compensate. The world is tired of our verbosity and only genuine compassion and radiant joy will communicate. If we are in touch with God in our own depths and truly in touch with ourselves, then the influence of our witness will communicate in ways undreamed of previously, and without our manipulation or interference.

There is a time for the prophetic word to be proclaimed, whether men will hear or reject, but we must be careful that it *is* the prophetic word and not some theological opinion or latest trendy fad of spirituality and party-line of our own devising.

It is required of us that we live our lives according to the Gospel, deepen our meditative experience of prayer saturated with scripture, so that the overflow of joy and love will obviously be relevant to the needs of those around us who lack meaning, enthusiasm and compassion.

Conclusion

Pulling the Threads Together

For us, the reading of the bible must not be the study of a dead letter, but encounter with the living Spirit. The Holy Spirit inspired the writers and inspires the reader. If we come to scripture appropriating the indwelling of the Spirit within our own heart, and if we prepare ourselves in body, mind and spirit, we shall enter into creative and profound experience of God.

Every part of our being should be dedicated to God. Physical awareness, imaginative vitality and spiritual illumination are all part of our life in God, and there is no area of our lives into which he cannot come with joy, enthusiasm and compassion.

If we bring the whole of ourselves into a meditative study of scripture, within a regular and disciplined period of quiet, then we shall know a continual awakening of the mind and heart which will sustain us in our daily discipleship and protect us in times of distress, darkness and conflict.

The Lord often visits the meditating believer with singular gifts of love and grace, though we can neither demand or command it. But we can request, expect and anticipate such grace. It may be that God will transform our meditation into contemplation, and we shall experience and glimpse that life of union which is under the direct control of the Holy Spirit, where we shall 'take off' not under our own exertion, but in the power and joy of God himself.

If scripture can thus be translated into our daily lives, it will be a source of sustaining joy to us, and infectious enthusiasm and tranquillity to those around us. God will be glorified in our own experience, in our life and witness to others, and through his word.

He will make the historic to become contemporary and relevant, 'for the word of God is living and active, sharper than any two-edged sword, piercing to the division of soul and spirit, of joints and marrow, and discerning the thoughts and intentions of the heart.' (Heb. 4:12).